MW01122181

Smile A While
A Treasury of Prince Edward Island Humour

ISBN-088882-107-7

Publisher: Anthony Hawke
Layout & design: Graphic Communications
Hounslow Press
A Division of Anthony R. Hawke Limited
124 Parkview Avenue, Willowdale, Ontario, Canada M2N 3Y5

Printed and bound in Canada

SMILE A WHILE

A Treasury of Prince Edward Island Humour

by Julie V. Watson

For our dreams............If we never build castles in the air, we shall never build them anywhere...........And there are some to build.

If we can't see the humour in life.......what enjoyment is there in dreams.....or building.

INTRODUCTION

When it was first suggested that I put together a book of Island humour my reaction was, no way. I can't write humour. I have a great admiration for the writer who can elicit a laugh, or even a giggle, from me when I'm reading, but know my own limitations in that area.

But then my friend, Molly who owns Down East Traditions, a gift shop at the CP Prince Edward Hotel in Charlottetown pointed out that travellers were always looking for collections of funny stories and jokes to help wile away the hours spent in a bus or hotel room. She knew I had found lots of funny stories during research for other books. And, she pointed out, I was always reminiscing about humourous incidents in our own lives.

I was thinking it over when something happened that made me roar with laughter and change my thinking:

We all do dumb things, since I spend so much time in the kitchen many of mine happen there. The coffee maker had been sending tantalizing aromas to me so I stopped work, grabbed a mug and proceeded to pour myself a coffee. I was so wrapped up in what I had been working on, I poured almost the whole cup before I realized the mug was upside down!

When I told a friend about it, she roared laughing too, my husband just grinned that funny smile he gives when I've done something else dumb.

That made me realize that life is full of humourous moments. Attentive ears and a dedication to jotting down one liners when I heard them, some incidents from our own life worth repeating and of course the wonderful little insights to life in times past that gave me the material that has been gathered into the collection. As well as giving me a laugh many of these chuckles have given me a good feeling about the continuity of life. Even in these fast paced modern times we still find the same things amusing, as was proven to me over and over again as I found the same jokes reappearing over the years. The telling may be a little different, but only slightly.

One of the best things this book could do is to trigger the readers minds to recall moments of humour from their own lives. Looking back on laughter shared with loved ones and friends is surely one of the most precious memories we can have.

Julie V. Watson

Julie V. Watson

Taking the license that is allowed all authors I am going to admit to self-indulgence and start this book with a couple of family stories.

CANVAS CAPERS

Camping was part of our life during the early years of our marriage. It was the only way we could afford to travel and we would often pack up our son, his friends, the two dogs and head out for adventures in new places. We met wonderful people, explored the country and really got to know the kids. Living in such close quarters leads to lots of communication, and teaches everyone how to compromise.

Ironically, now that we've marked our 25th, we've got back to camping with much less equipment and conveniences. The change came when we got back into motorcycle touring. We can only carry a small tent, sleeping bags, and minimal equipment on the bike, but find we love it anyway and are rediscovering the joys of nature, being outdoors and meeting like-minded people. But that's another story.

It was through camping that we discovered P.E.I. Those weeks in a tent at the North Shore so enthralled us that we moved here. Just like the guy and the razors, we liked it so much we bought it.

One incident on an early trip to P.E.I. stays in our minds. Our Welsh Corgi, Muggins, was just a pup. And as her name suggests she was a bit of a clown, always getting up to some mischief.

We had stopped at a farm to buy homemade bread, squares and a large coffee cake, then went to a store to get milk etc. In just minutes Muggins devoured the coffee cake, and was well into the squares when we got back to the car. Now to realize the implications of this you have to think in terms of sheer bulk. It was a large coffee cake, and with a half dozen squares was bigger than the little puppy. Expecting her to be sick we headed back to camp and tied her to a tree, well out of the way. This cute little tan coloured dog looked truly green by now and none too happy.

Jack, still annoyed, plunked her dinner and a bowl of water in front of her. "There you little glutton, lets see how hungry you are now," he snarled at her adding insult to her woes.

We presume it was the water that did it. Obviously in distress she lapped up too much too fast before we could get it way from her. Within minutes her tummy began to swell, soon she seemed bigger around than long. So swollen was she, laying down was impossible so there she sat. Obviously blaming Jack for her distress she staggered right to the end of her chain, as far from us as possible, turned her back and sat - suffering.

Till the day she died, some 17 years later, she would react to coffee cake in the same way. Jack would be treated to a turned back, and studiously ignored.

***

THE BRAWLEY BRUIN
AND THE BASEBALL BAT

Our family, extended by the addition of a niece, went camping in Jasper, Alberta. With two kids, two adults and the Corgis, Duchess and Muggins, we had travelled across the country and got our nightly routines down pat. Coolers

and all food were locked in the car trunk or left outside, both to keep the canvas on our tent trailer clean, and eliminate visits by wildlife in search of food while we were out or sleeping.

Entering Jasper we were reminded by National Park wardens of the presence of bears and elk, but were confident our camp habits would stand us in good stead. Even a huge elk, who came to lunch and greedily munched up all of our salad, didn't shake our smug feeling that we were doing everything right, and were in no danger at all. We were soon to learn a valuable lesson.

Just before dawn one morning the two dogs started whining to go out. Being a lover of early hours. I happily got up and took them with me on a walk through the campground to visit the washroom. On returning I tied them both to a tree and snuggled back into bed. It wasn't long before I realized all was not as it should be. The dogs were growling and snarling and I could hear a strange snuffling outside.

Quietly unzipping the window I peered out and was struck dumb. A huge brown bear was sitting outside, pawing our metal cooler out from under the cement picnic table. I woke Jack, then the kids. We carefully unzipped the door to the tent, and quietly evacuated. Jack brought up the rear; armed, he was prepared to defend his family. It would have been difficult, his "weapon" was a miniature kids baseball bat, about 14 inches long.

I meanwhile raced to a nearby metal house trailer and asked if we could come in. The lady smiled, and grinned. The kids had beaten me there, let themselves in and were bouncing by the window, screaming, "Save Duchess and Muggins Dad. please! please! Save them."

Knowing them to be safe I too armed myself - by grabbing her egg flipper - and headed back into the foray. The bear was not a happy bruin. Two yelping dogs were getting on his nerves. By now he had ripped the lid off the cooler, opened a plastic tub and eaten the butter. The rest of our food evidently did not meet his standards. He ignored it and turned to consider adding canine to his menu.

With encouragement from the kids, Jack, was trying to distract bruin's attention from the dogs by yelling and feinting with the baseball bat dodging to keep the car between them. Eventually I was able to dart in and unclip the leashes which were holding the dogs by the tree. Having more intelligence than the adults in the group, they too hightailed it for the house trailer and safety. We followed, hoping the bear would not do too much damage.

He didn't, with no crowd to admire his feats he seemed to loose interest and ambled off to repeat his cooler opening trick at another campsite where he helped himself to a ham before returning to the woods.

After a breakfast shared with other campers and we relived our adventures, we checked meticulously to see what had attracted the bear to our campsite. It was coconut. We had cracked a nut the night before and one of the kids forgetting the no food rule, had taken some to bed. One plus of this adventure was the rule-minding adulation from the kids who thought us heroes to have taken on a big brown bear, armed only with an egg flipper and fourteen inch toy baseball bat.

This was the second bear incident on that vacation. A week earlier, in Banff, the kids had returned from their routine chore of garbage disposal with the bag still in hand. Dad pooh poohed their excuse that there was "a bear in there", took the bag of garbage, opened the lid to the large container, and threw the garbage right in the face of an enraged black bear. Park officials handled that one by bringing in a fork lift and taking the container, plus bear, off to the dump.

***

Campers who arrive with a multitude of kids each with a bicycle (except baby who has a car seat and playpen), the dog, the cat, and two frazzled parents..... and one small tent trailer, are said to be - cramping out.

***

PONDEROUS PONG

The 10,000 Boy Scouts, leaders and volunteers who attended CJ'89, the Canadian jamboree held at Fort Amherst in 1989 awoke one morning to a "stink" which caused much guessing as to its origin.

"The tide's out and its seaweed rotting," guessed some. "Camp Caribou raided and turned over the outhouse," guessed the lads from Manitoba.

"Leader John should not have cooked up those beans last night," argued others.

The mystery was solved when the RCMP confirmed that a local farmer accidently dumped a load of rather liquid sheep manure along about 100 feet of the nearby highway. Traffic which had traveled through the mess spread its odiferous reminder far and wide even after the local fire department had sprayed the mess and cleaned the road.

It rained so hard at Cavendish that most campers packed up and left after four drenched days. Two teenagers, travelling on bicycles were invited by a local couple to move their things into a dry barn and sleep on the screened in porch.

"Thanks lady," grinned one wolfing down her offering of a hot supper in the farm kitchen, "we were starting to feel like we had taken up residence in a car wash."

SKYE PIONEERS

One of my favourite books about the history of Prince Edward Island is Skye pioneers and "The Island" by Malcolm A. Macqueen, probably published around 1929. Macqueen was a true storyteller whose prose gave us real insight into the life of his subjects. And indeed brought them to life for readers.

The following excerpts are not only humorous, but also give us a picture of the Skye Pioneers.

MERRY TWITTERINGS

"At a meeting of the elders of the Murray Harbor Road church, during the incumbency of Rev. Donald Macdonald, a complaint was lodged on behalf of some of the worshippers, that their minds were distracted during the sacred services by the twitterings of swallows nesting in the chimneys. Finally Mr. William Macphail was asked to "go on." Standing up before the assembled elders, and taking in his hands the ponderous Bible that was resting on the table, he allowed it to fall open where it would. It was understood that the chapter thus exposed to view was the one Divinely appointed to be read. When he had finished the lines "Yea, the sparrow hath found an house, and the swallow a nest for herself, where she may lay her young, even thine Altars, 0 Lord of Hosts, my King, and my God," the fate of the swallows was settled. After a brief prayer was said the meeting was dispersed. Until these cheerful visitors betook themselves to a sunnier home in the south their merry twittering was a part of each service as unfailing as the reading of Holy Writ itself."

DISHONORETH HER HEAD

Mrs. Mary J. MacLeod, widow of Rev. D.B. MacLeod of Orwell, on the death of her father was adopted by her relative Donald Joiner MacLeod, elder, of Kinross. Of the many customs which she recalls in this excellent household was that of the daily morning prayer. When Mr. MacLeod had the Bible ready, he called upon the women to cover their heads as enjoined by St. Paul: "Every woman that prayeth with her head uncovered dishonoreth her head (Cor. I,2.)." On these occasions the women present seized anything near at hand, such as an apron, men's hat, or any other object. On one occasion a lady visitor

who was not aware of the customs of the house, on being offered a bonnet, replied, "No thank you, my head is not cold."

THE LINER AND THE DOG

Mary Munroe MacSwain was interviewed for Skye Pioneers and "The Island". She had left her Highland home almost ninety years previously, and had a wealth of recall about the early days of Scottish immigrants in Prince Edward Island. We excerpted from her tale a story about the "liner" and the dog.

"With several neighbors we moved to the Head of Cardigan, then one of the most heavily wooded districts on the whole Island. No one can realize the toil involved in clearing the maples. The stumps never seemed to die. However, we stuck and this move proved our last. We liked to visit our old Brown's Creek neighbours, and we frequently drove across country on Saturday for the Sunday service, staying with friends over the weekend. Among the adherents of this congregation was William Lamont, the only member of that devoted church family not a follower of Reverend Donald Macdonald. Although not a gifted singer William Lamont was an expert liner. This was an important part of the precentor's duty, and it was well performed by him. At a time when each person the audience did not possess a book, it was necessary, if all were to sing, for someone at the beginning of each line or two to intone the words in a voice heard by the whole audience. This was known as lining. Once done each person had the words, and was thereby enabled to raise his voice in song. All sang, and sang fervently, and if all did not pray, those who did appropriated the time that would have been taken up by others had all prayed. The result was hearty, refreshing singing, and long tedious prayers. "On one of these occasions the Cardigan visitors were holding a service on Saturday evening at the home of one of their Brown's Creek friends. William Lamont was lining, and all present were entering with the greatest fervor into the song. It was fall, and

Boreas smote the log walls of the humble cottage with bitter blasts. The household dog had been driven from his accustomed haunt beside the open hearth, to make way for the press of visitors. Towards the end of the first song, a dismal howling was set up by the faithful Achates without, his spirit moved as much by the mournful and unusual harmony within, as by the bitter blasts without. At length the song was ended. The last note had scarcely died away before the precentor, in the same wavinging tone, and with the same fervid expression, carried on in Gaelic, Chaidh Satan a steach do'n choin' (Satan has entered into the dog). Thinking him still 'lining' the congregation, swept along by the enthusiasm of the occasion, took up the refrain, and from every throat there arose, loud in unison, 'Chaidh Satan a steach do n choin.' But if His Satanic Majesty had entered into the dog, as alleged by the respected precentor, his sojourn in the canine host was of short duration, for there was ample evidence in the frequent fistic encounters between the more quarrelsome members of the two rival religious factions*, at casual meetings over the flowing bowl, that he soon freed himself from the restraints of his shaggy habitation, and invaded the more congenial soil of the human heart."

* - The Free Church congregation founded by Scottish immigrants at Brown's Creek vs the neighbouring Established Church at Murray Harbour Road. After the "disruptions" which caused many good souls to leave their native Scotland for the Americas. "The newly arrived immigrants were keen partisans, and bitter foes of the Establishment," according to Mrs. MacSwain.

BESTS HIS MASTER

One Daniel McKinley was a preacher around the year 1853 who was perhaps overzealous about the subject of the believers immersion for baptism, instead of infant sprinkling. He preached it everywhere, but his favorite method was to attend the church services of other denominations and sit near the door in order to be first out. He took his stand outside and preached to the retiring congregation. To any question asked he was ready with a reply, frequently to the amusement of the assembled crowd. "On one occasion he attended the Murray Harbour Road church on Sacramental Sunday. Rev. Donald Macdonald, the minister, was conducting the service. McKinley began preaching by the roadside, and drew away some of the congregation from the service. Two of the elders advised him to desist. When he continued they carried him away bodily. In his clear sentorian voice, heard above the voice of the minister, conducting the service, he cried aloud, 'I am more highly honored than my Blessed Master. He was carried on one ass; I am carried on two.'"

STICKY WICKET

For the first few years after the church (at Orwell) was built, until permanent seats were installed, the congregation sat on planks placed for seats. Whatever these planks may have been they could not be more uncomfortable than the narrow straight-backed seats that were substituted for them. But this was not all. The painter, whoever he was, so mixed his materials that the worshippers stuck fast to the seat. Especially embarrassing was it for the ladies, who never knew whether their more delicate apparel would remain on themselves or adhere to the seat.

***

Did you hear about the bell ringer who got tangled up in the rope and tolled himself off.

***

UNITED COMPROMISE

In the good old days when Princetown was expected to live up to its reputation as a town, a log church was built down near the point. That was fine for people of that immediate neighbourhood, but for others who lived further away, it was not so convenient. Came the day when a new church was to replace the old. Came a time of argument and dissension. Those at the point wanted the church built there. Others wanted the church built at the quarry about five miles distant.

Those at the point won - temporarily. Up went the church framework.
Came a dark night!

9

The church was hastily loaded. There was a cracking of whips, a sense of victory, and the new church was off down the road. Meanwhile, the people of Princetown slumbered blissfully on, unconscious that their church was being taken for a ride.

Halfway to the quarry, the church compromised. It got stuck.

There it is still to-day, the Princetown United church.

Over On The Island
Helen Jean Champion1939

***

A new priest at his first mass was so scared he couldn't speak, let alone remember his sermon. The result was a stuttered dissertation few understood. Afterwards he asked the monsignor how he had done. The monsignor said fine, but next week it might help if you put a little vodka or gin in your water to relax you. The next week the priest put vodka in his water and really kicked up a storm. After mass he again asked the monsignor how he had done. The monsignor said "Fine, but there are some things you should get straight."

1. There are 10 commandments, not 12.
2. There are 12 disciples, not 10.
3. David slew Goliath, he didn't kick the shit out of him.
4. We do not refer to Jesus Christ as the "late J.C."
5. And next Sunday there is a taffy pulling contest at St. Peter's, not a peter pulling contest at St. Taffy's.
6. The Father, Son and Holy Ghost are not referred to as big daddy, junior and the spook."

K.M.

***

A farmer from up Tracadie Bay way was going to town on the morrow so he walked over and asked his neighbour if he would like to go along. Receiving a positive reply he told his neighbour he would be over at dawn, so as to be in town when the Co-Op opened. It was haying time and he could not afford to be away for long.

It was still dark when he knocked on his neighbours door the next morning. Half an hour later the sun was peeping over the horizon and he knocked again. Minutes later he rapped again. Then again, crying out that he would wait no longer than 5 minutes, or the cows would be coming home before they got away.

"Ach, for heaven's sake man be quiet or you'll wake the missus. I've been telling you for the past hour I'll be ready in a minute," was the irate reply.

***

Why did the farmer put hay under his pillow?
Because he wanted to feed his nightmare.

***

Suggested motto for the P.E.I. Oldtime Woodsmen Association: "Armstrong Power"

***

What do you get when you cross 500 pigs with 500 deer?
Sows 'n' bucks

***

What do you get when you cross a potato and a sponge?
I don't know but it sure soaks up a lot of gravy.

***

Why did they bury the farmer under the oak tree?
Because he was dead.

***

Did you hear about the matron who went to pick her pail of milk up from the farmer. She found a bee in it and turned to him to ask how such a thing could have happened."It must've flew in one ear and out the udder!"

***

One of the farms great mysteries is why a hay baler that has been allowed to rest all winter refuses to work come spring.

***

THE BULL IN THE HILLSBOROUGH BRIDGE

This is a true story related to me by Walter O'Brien, a Charlottetown writer "for the papers" who made my early days at the Guardian just a little bit more fun with all his tales. He says this is a true story.

"When the old Hillsborough Bridge was brought here from New Brunswick it had a draw in the center that could be opened to allow ships to pass up or down the river. There was a man to operate the draw when necessary. He had a small shack in the center of the bridge to live in. The man was a Mr. Docherty from the Vernon River section.

"Down on East Grafton Street at the railway crossing there was a large cattle pen where Canada Packers stood. This mighty yard was used to hold cattle for shipment or slaughter. One day there was a farmer who had a large bull in the waiting pen. He noticed the animal was ill and he called the vet or doctor who said the animal would need an enema. He did not have his equipment with him at the time but said if he had one of those old long dinner horns he could do the job.

"Someone came up with the so called horn and things were got ready. The bull was led by the farmer to a given spot in the pen when all was ready by the vet. He put the end of the horn in the bulls rear end and was about to pour the mixture in when the bull went mad and broke away from the farm and ran away towards the old bridge. The horn started to blow and the faster the bull ran the louder the horn would blow.

"Mr. Docherty the bridge attendant heard the loud horn and said its the ships whistle. He opened the draw to let her through, but instead of a ship or ferry the large bull tumbled into the opening, with the horn in his rear still blowing loud and long, and was lost.

"The farmer was so enraged he said that a man attending the draw in the bridge who did not know a horn in a bull's ass from a ships whistle should be fired from the bridge job and made to pay for the lost animal.

This is a true story called 'the bull in the bridge'."

Walter O'Brien

***

*Rural communities have numerous small rituals that mark the seasons. One in our neighbourhood occurs each fall. The approaching winter inspires property cleanup resulting in small gatherings at the community dumpsters. So popular is our community dump that you occasionally have to line up as, we did on a Sunday in a recent November.

Of course the first thing that ninty percent of the populace does is take a look in the bins in anticipation of finding some item of indescribeable value - at the very least a piece of antique furniture that just needs a spit and polish. HOW we convince ourselves that the previous score and four people there before us overlooked it I'm not sure.

Conversation depends heavily on the content of your load. Old limbs, leaves, house junk and such brings forth a "Fixin' the yard ayeh."

Molding hay or straw, rotted off fence posts and rusted barb wire will inspire such remarks as, "Fixin' the barn ayeh."

Talk often turns to the weather, which if foul can occupy many minutes with reminisces of other years when conditions were surely ten times worse than in this era of soft, pampered young folk - even on days when we stand gasping for breath after pushing and pulling our bags of garbage through snowdrifts up to our crotch all the way in from the road.

Then there is the old standby conversation opener, "How are you today?" or "How are you Keepin?" A typical response:

"I'm not so sure. Get up in the morning and look in the obit column. If I'm not there I's keeps goin ."

***

An Islander was invited to speak to a banquet in Ontario. He became more and more upset as speaker after speaker told tall tales of Ontario's fishing industry.

Then at last the visitor from Canada's "Garden of the Gulf" was asked for a few remarks.

"Well we don t have any fish on P.E.I. worth bragging about," he began humbly, then holding his hands about twelve inches apart, "I never say any bigger than that."

Surveying those gathered, he paused, then smirked, "Of course, you'll have to remember that we always measure our fish between the eyes."

Red & White, Autumn '52

***

A: (relating some of his naval experiences)... and then the Captain staggered in and shouted: "The ship has sprung a leak."
I: "And what did you do?"
A: "I told him to put a pan under it and go back to bed."

Red & White, Winter '48

***

15

People have been wondering for ages why it is that crabs walk sideways. Well, it's like this: a crab, having once got a look at himself in the mirror gave such a violent shrug that forever after he doesn't give a hang where he's been, or where he is going, and therefore moves in the only other direction he knows of.

A father crab once said to his son: "Young un unless you larn your books you'll never get aside in the world."

Red & White, Winter 49

***

Friend: "I heard you buried your wife, old chap."
Sailor: "I had to — dead you know."

***

Two fishermen went out jigging for cod and had a really great haul which filled the boat.
"Gee," said one, "this is a real great spot. We'd better mark it so we can find it tomorrow."
"Right," agreed his buddy," leaning over to mark an 'X' on the side of the boat.

Carol Rogers

Then there was the fisherman's wife who sent the old handyman down to the docks to get a mackerel for supper. He fell down dead.
"What did you do then?"
"I opened a can of tuna."

***

A fisherman from North Cape had long expressed the desire to be buried at sea when the time came for him to go to his Maker. Finally the inevitable happened and his sons and nephews were determined to fulfill the old mans wish. Only trouble was, the lads had an awful time digging his grave.

***

A ship of dreams sometimes may be a ship in distress on the ocean of miscalculations.

John of the Lilacs
Golden Moments

***

A guy from Murray River decided to go ice fishing. He cut a hole in the ice, but before he could get a worm on his hook a voice boomed out, "There's no fish here."

So he moved and cut another hole. But again, he didn't get his line baited before a voice yelled out, "There's no fish here."

Being a persistent fellow, he moved again, and cut another hole. Again he was stopped by the authoritative voice. "God?" he questioned looking up."

"No, you fool," came the reply. "It's the rink attendant."

***

Lucy Maud Montgomery

No book written about P.E.I.'s people would be complete without mention of Lucy Maud Montgomery, P.E.I.'s most famous daughter of the letters, best known for her novel Anne of Green Gables. In the fall of 1901 Lucy Maud went to Halifax where she worked on the Staff of the Daily Echo, the evening edition of the Chronicle. As is often the case with new employees she was put to a number of tasks including proofreading and..."On Saturdays the Echo has a lot of extra stuff, a page of 'society letters' among the rest. It usually fell to my lot to edit these. Can't say I fancy the job much, but the only thing I positively abhor is 'faking' a society letter. When a society letter fails to turn up from a certain place — say from Windsor — in due time, the news editor slaps a Windsor weekly down before me and says blandly, 'Fake up a society letter from that, Miss Montgomery."

The youthful "newspaper woman" was able to see humour of her situation, even when given such a tedious task as this excerpt from an article she wrote for the September, 1917 edition of Everywoman's World magazine in which she quoted from her journals, proves.

"Palmday, May 3, 1902.

"I spent the afternoon expurgating a novel for the news-editor's use and behoof. When he was away on his vacation his substitute began to run a serial in the Echo called "Under the Shadow." Instead of getting some A.P.A. stuff as he should have done, he simply bought a sensational novel and used it. It was very long and was only about half done when the news-editor returned. So, as it would run all summer, in its present form, I was bidden to take it and cut mercilessly out all unnecessary stuff. I have followed instructions, cutting out most of the kisses and embraces, two-thirds of the love-making, and all the descriptions, with the happy result that I have reduced it to about a third of its normal length, and all I can say is "Lord, have mercy on the soul of the compositor who has to set it up in its present mutilated condition."

Saturday, May 31, 1901.

"I had a good internal laugh to-night. I was in a street car and two ladies beside me were discussing the serial that had just ended in the "Echo". 'You know' said one, 'it was the strangest story I ever read. It wandered on, chapter after chapter, for weeks, and never seemed to get anywhere; and then it just finished up in eight chapters, "licketty-split". I can't understand it!"

"I could have solved the mystery, but I didn't"

Note: "A.P.A." stuff refers to editorial material that can be purchased from a wire service. I presume the discrepancy in dates was a typographical error in Everywoman!

***

Anyone who has any acquaintance with Lucy Maud knows of her active imagination and ability to build wonderous tales of fantasy. It is natural that she should be intrigued with such things as ghosts and wraiths. This lass with the fertile mind loved the shivery feeling of being spooked. She related one tale of her friend Dave who joined her in the apple orchard one evening, whispering of hearing bells ringing in a desserted house. "To be sure the marvellous edge was soon taken off," when it was found to be a newly-cleaned clock striking the hours. She savoured such experiences though, and often used them in her writing. The bell incident became the foundation of the "Ghostly Bell" chapter in another book, "The Story Girl." But one night Lucy Maud and her faithful friends had a real ghost scare — "the real qualifying scare, not ghost."
They were playing at twilight in a hayfield near the house, chasing each other around the "fragrant coils of new-cut hay," when she glanced in the direction

of the orchard dyke. "A chill began galloping up and down my spine, for there, under the juniper tree, was really a white thing, shapelessly white in the gathering gloom." It could be Mag Laird, a local beggar, they thought; or perhaps a white calf. But no, it was definetly a "white thing," and worse it seemed to be "after us at last."

The three fled to the house, seeking refuge in her grandmother's bedroom. She was not where expected, so they took flight again, to a neighbours "trembling in every limb." There they gulped out their tale only to be ridiculed for their nonsense, especially after servants checked on the "white thing" and found nothing there.

Lucy Maud of course, knew there would be nothing there, such apparitions would only appear to fulfill their mission of scaring three wicked children out of their senses and then vanish. "But go home we would not until Grandfather appeared and marched us back in disgrace. For what do you think it was?

A white tablecloth had been bleaching on the grass under the juniper tree, and, just at dusk, Grandmother, knitting in hand, went out to get it. She flung the cloth over her shoulder and then her ball fell and rolled over the dyke. She knelt down and was reaching over to pick it up when she was arrested by our sudden stampede and shrieks of terror. Before she could move or call out we had disappeared.

So collapsed our last "ghost" and spectral terrors languished after that, for we were laughed at for many a long day."

***

AMBASSADOR

I must tell my own favourite "Anne" experience. Flying from Charlottetown to Vancouver to attend a writers convention, the same year that Expo turned Vancouver into party city, I boarded a 747 in Toronto that had every seat booked - most of them with tourists from Japan.

I took my seat, a window with one seat beside me, then the aisle. Beside me was an elderly lady, whose husband was seated across the aisle. He immediately closed his eyes and dropped off to sleep. As we settled into our seat I said hello. She smiled, shyly dropped her eyes and replied in Japanese, seeming embarrased because we did not share a language, and also very tired.

She seemed a little nervous so I perservered mentioning Vancouver and Expo. She smiled. I pointed to her and said "Japan." She nodded and smiled again. I pointed to myself and said Prince Edward Island.

Her tired face lit up. "Anne of Green Gables," she excitedly asked. I nodded. She grabbed her husband and shook him. Pointing at me she cried "Anne of Green Gables."

She reached around the seat to the person in front, pointed and cried, "Anne of Green Gables."

From that moment on the chatter increased among the weary Japanese tour group. For the rest of the flight every time one of their number passed our seat she would chatter, point to me a beam, "Anne of Green Gables."

I was a celebrity. Smiles, nods and confirmation of a relationship with "Anne" which I am sure had become greatly exagerated by now, even followed me to the washroom.

Some members of the group even came up and shook my hand as we waited for the luggage to come down to the carousel after arriving at Vancouver. I had to explain that it was not my fame as an author that was causing the excitment, afterall my couple of cookbooks hardly gained me international attention. Instead I was basking in the glory of another Island author, Lucy Maud Montgomery.

Still it was a fun way to start a visit!

***

LOGIC

This is supposedly a true story from the early days of medicine which was passed on through a Dr. A.A. MacDonald in the early 60's.

Dr. Dockerty of Cape Traverse had a sense of humor. His horse spilled him out of his sleigh one day and Dockerty picked up his buffalo robe...shoved his fur cap on a bit firmer and started trudging down the road carrying the robe. He was met by a farmer in a wood sleigh who asked, "Is that your horse running away?"

"No, No, the doctor said soothingly..."he's running home."

Dockerty claimed to be the first to operate on appendix on the Island...A lot of puss had formed around the appendix of a patient...He ran into it/turned the woman on her belly with a drain and let it drain out...She got better.

***

A farmer who had been under the weather was finally convinced to go to town and visit the doctor. On returning home he assured his wife that he was not seriously ill, but she could sense that he was deeply troubled and pressured him to tell her what was wrong.

"She said I should take one of these pills every day for the rest of me life," he said holding up a vitamin. "So what's wrong," she asked.

He sniffed, "She only gave me four pills!"

Overheard on the media bus during a Royal Tour

***

MALPEQUE CURE

Residents of Malpeque have a cure for coughs caused by the common cold: Take two Exlax before going to work. You won't dare cough all day.

Beth Smith, Kensington

Pulling the small boy out of a hole in the frozen-over pond, the man asked, "How did you come to fall in?"

"I didn't come to fall in!" the boy gasped, pushing himself to his feet, "I came to skate."

M.G. - Alexandra

***

OLD AGE IS. .....

When just about everything hurts and what doesn't hurt -doesn't work.
When you sit in your rocking chair and can't get it started.
When you sink your teeth into a steak and they stay there.
When your arms are too short to read the paper.
When you suddenly notice that your children are beginning to look middle-aged.
When the little old lady you help across the street is your wife.

The Venerables - via
Debbie Gamble Arsenault

***

'TIS THE BEST OF GIN

"A novel enterprise that was undertaken in the mid-seventies ended in the late eighties (1870-1889) when the Scott Act intervened. This was the distillery of Martin McInnis located within the confines of the village (St. Peters). Here in the West End he erected a building, and installed vats and machinery, and using molasses which was landed on the South Side Wharf in huge puncheons, fermented and distilled a potent rum, sold in taverns from Charlottetown to East Point. In connection with this Martin McInnis, and with the readers forbearance, we will relate an incident, which no doubt he along with us considered amusing and entertaining. Two local characters, who had never probed the mysteries of the printed word, found a bottle half full with a colorless liquid, smelling good but which they were afraid to drink without authoritive direction. Now as Martin was known to be an authority on all things alcoholic, they decided to take the bottle to him for on the spot analysis. Martin uncorked the bottle, smelled its contents, shook his head and took a speculative swallow. Again he shook his head, again sniffed and drank a couple of large swallows. He looked thoughtful for a moment, then tipped up the bottle and drained the liquid therein, threw down the now empty container into the gutter stating empirically, "The best of Holland Gin" to the disgruntled pair."

from A Brief History of
St. Peter's Bay by
C.C. Pratt - a delightful wee book of reminicance

***

Two men were standing outside the Charlottetown Post Office discussing the postal service. "It's awful what they charge these days," said one. "Why it costs 38 cents just to send a letter to Cornwall."

After much thought his friend said, "Well, that's not so bad considering it works out to only about a penny a day."

M.G. - Alexandra

NONSENSE AVENUE AT S.D.U.

St. Dunstan's University is part of Charlottetown's heritage, and one fondly remembered by many local folk. Although St. Dunstan's has been replaced by the University of Prince Edward Island, its memory lives on, triggered by copies of the old Red and White, the college magazine for S.D.U. The following excerpts are from the section "The Funny Man" which later became "Nonsense Avenue", surely a favourite with student readers. As one editor put it -

(Please note. The characters used in this section are purely ludicrous. Any similarity to the names of persons living or nearly dead is absolutely preconceived)

***

A CASE OF UNREMITTING KINDNESS

Cliff: "I understand your father is a very kind man, he writes to you nearly every mail."
Polar: "When he don't send a cheque, do you call it kindness?"
Cliff: "Sure! Unremitting kindness."

***

Billy: "They say he has more money than he knows what to do with."
Creamer: "Ah, such ignorance must be bliss!"

***

PATRIOTIC

Mellady: "What is your impression, when you see the flag of your country waving over your head?"
Livy: "My impression is that it's blowing."

***

HISTORY HELPS

Prof: "To aid your memory I will give you Columbus dates in a little rhyme,
'Columbus sailed the ocean blue
In the year fourteen ninety-two' —
Repeat it."
St. Clair: "Columbus sailed the dark blue sea
In the year fourteen ninety three!"

(June, 1915)

27

Doc Bird Says:-

"Good friends, you can see that we wish to amuse,
Tho' some may not fance the means that we use;
If the joke on yourself, then, no pleasure should lend—
Why, laugh till you split at the joke on your friend."

***

Business Manager: "Well, John, how many orders did you get today?"
Creamer: "I got two orders in one place!"
Bus. Mgr.: "That's the stuff, what were they?"
Creamer: "One was to get out and the other, to stay out."

***

Prof. "What is a vacuum?"
Finol: "I know pere, I have it in my head, but I can't express it'"

***

Valley: "The dentist told me I had a large cavity that needed filling."
Bunny: "Did he recommend any special course of study?"

***

Fair One: "What a pity it is that handsome men are always so awfully conceited?"
Russel: "Not always, my dear, I'm not."

***

Harrigan: "Here waiter there is a fly in my soup!"
Jasper: "Serves the brute right. He's been buzzing around here all morning."

(December, 1915)

***

John: "Did you know that I was a life saver last summer?"
Leo: "Really, what flavour?"

***

Danny: "Are you fond of Dogs?"
Margaret: "If you mean that as a proposal you'd better ask papa."

28

Mother sent John and baby into the garden to play, but it was not long before cries disturbed her.

"John, what is wrong with the baby now?", she inquired from her washtub.

"I don't know what to do with him, Mother," replied John. "He's dug a hole and wants to bring it into the house."

***

S. D. U. STUDENT'S PHILOSOPHY

As I sit here,
Eyes like lead,
I wish that I
Were tucked in bed.

I throw my books,
Tear off my clothes,
Jump into bed,
Begin to doze;
Exams real soon,
Hang that warning —
I'm safe with Morpheus
Until morning.

(Winter, 1948)

CUSS NOAH, ANYWAY

We mortals have to swat and shoo
The flies from dawn to dark,
Cause Noah didn't swat the two,
That roosted in the Ark.

***

NOW IT CAN BE KNOWN

For the past eight months there have been secret meetings on the campus that have caused a lot of concern to the students. In short this secret can now be told to the public. A group of energetic students have carefully gathered and compiled the following astounding information. Through hard work and ceaseless difficulties they struggled on — we wonder why! This is the result:

A synonym is a word you use when you can't spell the word you thought you'd use instead of the one you have already used.

An optimist is a man who does a crossword puzzle with a fountain pen.

The sweetest memories in life are the recollections of things forgotten.

A clay pipe has been found to be the handiest for all around use. One convenient feature is that when you drop it, you never have to pick it up.

It is said that everything comes to him that waits. But in the refectory we notice that he who doesn't wait gets his first.

(Spring, 1949)

NOW LOOK WHAT THEY HAVE GONE AND DONE

Marketed helium capsules for people who find it difficult to get up in the morning.

Shipped mud pies to underprivileged children who live in rocky localities.

Raised cantaloupes than can.

Produced prepared beach lunches with a nice grade of sharp white sand already in the sandwiches.

Devised a sun tan with a zipper, to be slipped on by tourists who go to Florida for a vacation and spend all their time in the nightclubs.

***

Adam and Eve were naming the animals of the earth, when a hippopotamus strolled past.

"Well darling," said Adam, "what are we going to call that?"

"I know," said Eve, "let's call it a hippopotamus."

"But why?" asked Adam.

"Well," said Eve, "it looks more like a hippopotamus than anything we've named so far."

***

Bun: "From the looks of you there might have been a famine."
Lannan: "Yes, and by the looks of you, you might have caused it."

31

S.D.U. FICTIONARY

ARKUPATION — Noah's job during the flood.
LOCKSURIOUS — A nice head of hair.
PERHAPSODY - A musical improvisation with possibilities.
WRISTAURANT — Food on the cuff.
SNOEL — A white Christmas.

(Winter, 1949)

EPITAPH

Here lies an Atheist
All dressed up and no place to go.

***

John was trying to have his little joke at the expense of Jesse.
"Where were you born?" he asked Jesse. "Bloomfield!"
"Whatever for?" John asked wittily.
"At such a time," Jess answered, "It was my dutiful wish to be with my mother!"

***

"Mrs. Clancy, your child is spoiled!"
"Mrs. O'Brien, don't you dare say a thing like that about my child!"
"Mrs. Clancy, it's the truth. With my own eyes, I just saw a big truck run over him and he's entirely spoiled."

***

"Niver fear, Pat; shure, yez have a upright judge to thry ye."
"Ah, Biddy darlin', the devil an upright judge I want. Tis wan that'll lane a little."

***

During the depression years, a little girl was born in Charlottetown and her folks went down to the registration office to get her a birth certificate. The clerk asked the child's name.
"Stephanie Wilema Lelila MacDonald."
Clerk: "More paper, please."

***

32

"Has Pat been taking the medicine I prescribed?" the doctor asked, "— a tablet before each meal and a small whisky after?"

"Well, Doctor, maybe he's a few tablets behind; but he's months ahead on the whisky!"

(Spring, 1950)

A travelling salesman, having missed his train, found himself with two hours to spend in a small village. He approached an ancient resident:

Traveller: "Got a theatre here?"

Resident: "Nope."

Traveller: "A pool-room or library?"

Resident: "Nope."

Traveller: "Well how on earth do you amuse yourselves?" Resident: "We go down to the general store in the evenings — they have a new bacon slicer there."

***

Said one cannibal to the other: "Who was that lady I saw with you at the picnic?"

"That was no lady" replied the other, "that was my lunch."

Autumn, 1950

***

What follows was overheard in Dalton Hall during the mad preparations that always preceed a night in town.

Big Tom: "I've got to be at the corner of Queen and Richmond Street at seven o'clock, to pick up my girl for the dance.

Curley: "Who is it this time?"

Big Tom: "How should I know who'll be at the corner of Queen and Richmond at seven O'clock?

***

GUARANTEE

At a local drug store John was inquiring about the prices of perfumes. "It's my girl friend's birthday and I want to get her something real nice," he told the clerk.

The clerk showed John a number of different brands but he could not be satisfied. In exasperation the clerk went in back and when he returned he had a small vial. "Now here's something that'll make a real gift," he beamed as John examined the vial, "It's called 'Perhaps'. It s thirty-five dollars an ounce."

"Thirty-five dollars an ounce," exclaimed John, "For thirty-five dollars I don't want 'Perhaps'. I want 'Sure'."

***

The eighth Duke of Devonshire once told some friends: "The other night I dreamed I was addressing the House of Lords. Then I woke up and, by George, I was."

***

Commencing a discussion having to do with the Atomic Theory the Father wrote an equation on the board and stated that a certain number of electrons were involved. From this he developed an entire board full of equations, winding up at the bottom with: "So you see we have five less electrons than at the start. What has become of them?"

Not a sound was heard from the class. Imperiously the Father asked again: "Gentlemen, where are those electrons?" It was time for action and from a rear seat came a gruff command: "Don't nobody leave dis room!"

***

Concluding, we would like to remind all of the one about the Australian who bought a new boomerang because he got tired throwing the old one away.

***

Here Endeth The Humour Section.

(Spring, 1951),

***

PHEW

The social tyrant of the Senior Class, was engaged in conversation with a sweet young thing at the social one Thursday when she asked: "Why don t you get more late permissions?"

34

"It's the Rector. He just can't seem to understand that we should spend more time in town. He's become very difficult as of late and he doesn't seem to want to do anything about it. He's unreasonable and completely devoid of any sympathetic feelings towards the socialites of the college. He's just heartless.

Sweet Young Thing: "Do YOU know who I am?"

"Well?"

Sweet Young Thing: "I'm the Rector's niece."(after a painful silence of several seconds, summing up all the indignation he could) "Do YOU know who I am?"

Sweet Young Thing: "No, I don t."

"Thank heaven!" said the senior and took the next taxi back to the college.

***

Murphy and his lady fair were sitting at the dance one night having a heart to heart talk. "Suppose you had money", the lady cooed, "What would you do?" Murph drew himself up to his full height and, to impress her with his masculinity, he boasted: "I'd give in to the wanderlust. I'd live the rugged life of an adventurous soldier of fortune, leaving home never to return again." He felt her warm hand slide into his. He paused for a moment, looked up and found she was gone... and in his hand was a dime.

***

PUN PRO

What follows was submitted by a professional punster, who, of late, has been confined to an insane asylum with an incurable occupational neurosis. It is dedicated to all those who hold that the pun is the most sparkling form of wit.

A professor of Greek tore his suit and took it to a tailor names Acidopulus, from Athens. Mr Acidopolus examined the suit, and aksed, "Euripides?"

"Yes," said the professor, "Eumendes?"

(Winter, 1951)

"Today my heart beat 103,389 times, my blood travelled 168,000,000 miles, I breathed 23,040 times, I inhaled 438 cubic feet of air, I spoke 4,800 words, moved 750 major muscles, and I exercised 7,000,000 brain cells. I'm tired.

***

"I got up at dawn to see the sun rise," boasted a student.

"Well," commented another, "you couldn't have chosen a better time."

***

Assistant editor of a High School paper, was captured by a band of cannibals and interviewed by the cannibal chief, who happened to be an Oxford graduate:

"And what is your occupation?" inquired the chief hungrily.

"I'm on the staff of High School paper."

"Are you an editor?" drooled the chief.

"No, but I'm an assistant editor."

"Let me be the first to congratulate you on your impending promotion. After dinner you'll be an editor in chief."

(Spring, 1952)

This little poem was dedicated to Father R. during his illness:

0 I C
I'm in a 10 der mood today
& feel poetic, 2;
4 fun I'll just — off a line
& send it off 2 U.

I'm sorry you've been 6 so long
Don't B disconsol 8
But bear you ills with 42de
& they won t seem so gr 8.

contributed by a Math 1 student.

MITCHELL

A man named MacDonald warned his teen-age daughter, a co-ed at St. Dunstan's, that she was getting too many telephone calls from her boy friend. She instructed her swain that if her father answered, he was to ask for some fictitous person and pretend he had the wrong number.

After a few such calls the father decided to have a bit of fun with the next caller. The conversation went like this. Voice on the phone - "Ah - - - Mr. Mitchell?"

Mr. MacDonald - "That's right."

A silence, then the voice a little puzzled inquired: "Is this Mr. A.J. Mitchell?"

Mr. MacDonald - "That's right."

Another second of silence, then,

"Is this the A.J. Mitchell of the law firm?"

A full minute of silence, then,

"Sorry, Mr. MacDonald, but you're not the Mitchell I wanted to talk to."

***

ODE TO A FROG

What a wonderful bird the frog are—
When he stand he sit almost;
When he hop, he fly almost.
He ain't got no sense hardly;
He ain't got no tail hardly either.
When he sit, he sit on what he ain't got almost.

Anonymous

Girls like a strong silent boy friend because they think he is listening.

***

FROG WITCH

The other afternoon in Biology Lab. Edward Dalton encountered a human skeleton and in a fit of poetic passion composed this cadaverous verse:
It's hard to think
Albert true
That without flesh
I'd be like you.

And harder still
To think ol' pal
That one of these
Fine days I shall.

***

And when Noreen Connolly described a cow followed by two ducks as — milk and quackers — we decided it was time to sign off. - Editors.
In closing, it is only fitting that we close.

(Autumn, 1952)

While Father Arsenault was arranging material in the reading room for an art display, Moses Coady walked up to him and pointing to a picture said, "And this, I suppose is one of those hideous caricatures you call modern art?"

"No," replied Fr. Arsenault, "that's a mirror."

***

Billy, while going into Memorial Hall one afternoon, noticed a truck driver struggling unsuccessfully with a heavy case of books. "I'll give you a hand," volunteered Billy. The two seized opposite end of the case and huffed and puffed for several minutes to no avail.

"I'm afraid it is hopeless," said the despairing Bill. "We'll never get it on the truck."

"On," screamed the driver, "I'm trying to get it off."

***

WONDERS

Just recently Don McCarron was enjoying the wonders of Tignish as pointed out by Leonard Shea, a native of the place:

"What beautiful turnips!" exclaimed Don as he passed a large garden.

"Turnips," came the startled answer, "Those are just small potatoes."

"And what are those enormous blossoms in the field?"

"Oh, just dandelions," replied Len with a bored yawn.

A few moments later they were driving along the shore-line overlooking Northumberland Strait.

"Ah," noted Don smoothly, "I see someone's radiator is leaking."

***

John Clarkin, the poet-laureate of third corridor Memorial Hall coined this masterpiece,

> Roses are Red,
> Violets are blue
> I wanted some milk
> And the cow came through.

***

The other evening Fr. C. caught some of the students raising a rumpus in one of the rooms. He proceeded to lay down the following restrictions: "No more card playing. No more radios. No more shouting in the corridors. No more loud talk during study, etc. etc. etc." After he had finished, an imposing silence fell

across the room. It was broken by a timid voice belonging to C.K. who ventured, "Father, - - - uh - - -, if you don't mind my pen scratches a little."

(Winter, 1952)

Father E peered over his glasses at his students and said, "The time has come to dissect a frog. I have one in my pocket for the experiment." He took a crumbled paper bag out of his pocket and extracted from it a very tired-looking cheese sandwich. Trembling visibly, Father E. ejaculated, "Good Heavens, I distinctly remember eating my lunch."

***

The Rector and the Bursar were discussing what they would like to do in their old age.
Rector: "I would like to be superintendent of an orphanage. Then I wouldn't get any letters from parents."
Bursar: "I have a much higher ambition. I want to be warden of a penitentiary, because the alumni never come back to visit.

(Spring, 1953)

***

WRECK

The editors explained to reader of this issue that a joke is not a thing but a process, a trick you play on the reader's mind. You start him off towards a plausible goal, and then by a sudden twist you land him nowhere at all — or just where he didn't expect to go.

"When I first came to this country I didn't have a nickel in my pocket — now I have a nickel in my pocket."

That is one of the briefest jokes we can think of, yet shows the two parts of which all jokes are composed: the dispatch and the wreckage of a train of thought.

***

Then there is the story of the professor who dreamed he was lecturing to his class, and woke up to find that it was true.

***

A guy is wandering around with amnesia, trying to find out who he is. He meets a pretty girl who says: "I don't know who I am either — I was left on a doorstep." "Maybe you're a bottle of milk."

***

A lawyer upon reaching his office one morning found his faithful janitor sprawled over the door-step dead. He ran to the inner office and there found his secretary bound to a chair. The office showed signs of a desperate search; he precious files were strewn about the room, and a bottle of ink was spilled on the floor.

"What on earth has happened?" exclaimed the lawyer. "It was Sam. He has shot the janitor and he's looting the vault right now."

The lawyer rushed into his vault and there, sure enough was his friend Sam from Czechoslovakia.

"Why, Sam," he cried, almost bursting into tears, "how could you do this to me? Didn't I rescue you from the clutches of Adolph Hitler? And now you repay me by coming to my office and spilling ink over my linoleum."

You laugh at this because your expectations were tense and dramatic, and the collapse is complete. The joke is on you. All jokes — no matter whom else they are on, are on the person who laughs.

(Winter, 1953)

The optimist fell ten stories,
At each window bar
He shouted to his friends,
"All right so far."

THE NOSE KNOWS

Walter Bell had a big nose. Mrs. Quinlan had a big nose. And they were very bad friends.

One day they met on a bridge, Walter held his nose over the side of the bridge and said, "Can we pass." She was wild at the implied insult that her nose would get in the way.

Albert Muttart, Carleton August, 1955

FELINE STRIPES

Then there was the story of David and Yvonne Bradshaw, of McCrady's Green Acres in Meadowbank, which appeared in a British magazine called Residentia Abroad. The couple came to Canada when David retired after 25 years service as a master chef in the British Army. They purchased McCrady's, a restaurant and motel, and settled in to enjoy life in rural Prince Edward Island. Severe winters and encounters with four-footed residents have made the experience - interesting.

In the article David related the story of feeding the family cats.

"We have a black one and a white one. I thought I was seeing things. Another one, half black and half white, was in feeding between them. I noticed a funny smell, and realized the middle one wasn't a cat at all."

***

Following the bankruptcy of their neighbour a farmer and his missus were going over the books to see if they would be able to hang on for another year. In disgust the farmer threw down his pen, and turned off the calculator.

"Well, there it is in black and white," he sighed. "We're in the red."

Commiserated his wife with a sigh, "I'm afraid poverty is catching. You get it from politicians."

Debbie Gamble Arsenault

***

STRONG WIND

Another old timer suffered terrible from "gut gas" and went to the doctor who told him he had to watch his diet and give up the spicy food he loved. The stubborn old coot would not follow the doctors instructions and went back time and time again. He tried pills, and tonics to no avail. Finally he went back again.

"Doctor, Doctor. You've got to give me something for this wind!" he cried.

The doctor, tired of the demands from a patient who refused to do anything to help himself, muttered, "I'll give you exactly what you deserve," and handed the patient a kite.

***

Follow your knows: not what someone else thinks he knows, then your nose will not be pushed out of place.

John of the LilacsGolden Moments,

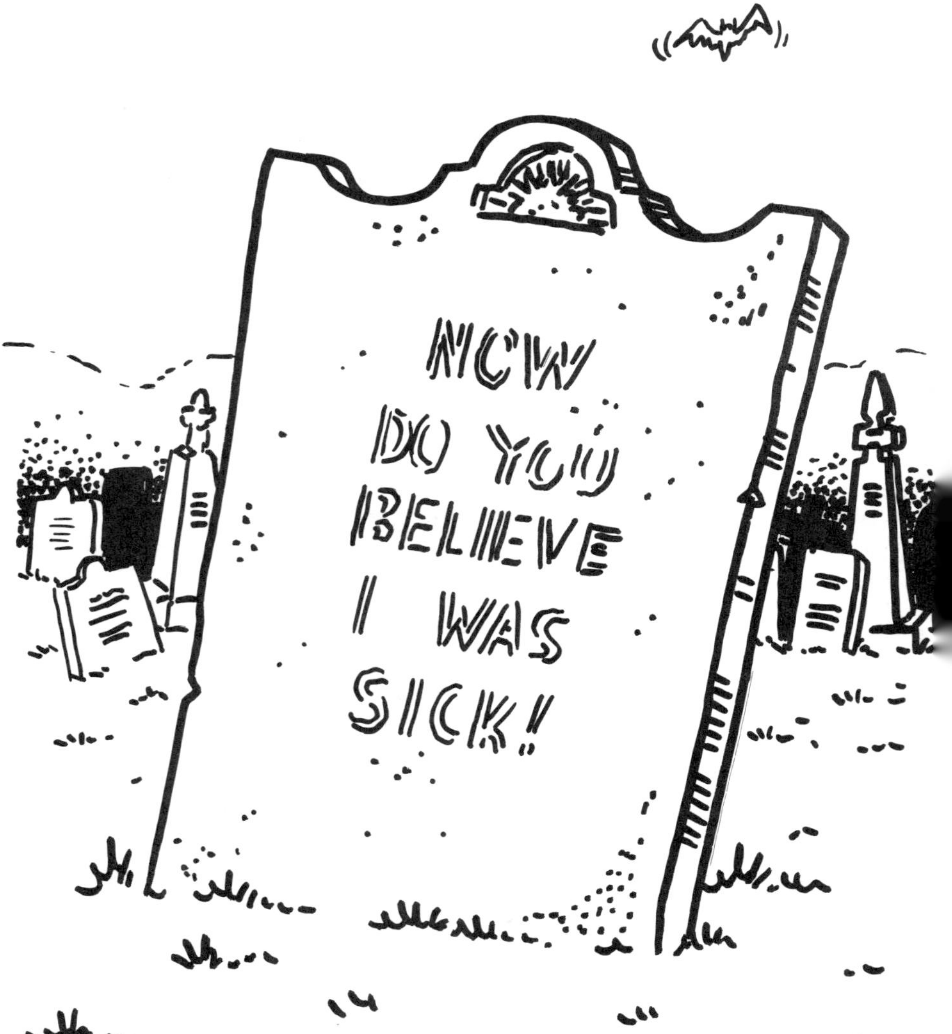
NOW
DO YOU
BELIEVE
I WAS
SICK!

Then there was the hypochondriac from Summerside. After years of his complaints and imaginary illnesses no one would pay him much mind anymore. Of course he did eventually become ill, but could get no sympathy and knew he would die alone and uncared for. Determined to leave his mark he wrote his own epitaph and had it put on his tombstone.

"NOW do you believe I was sick!"

***

A U.S. politician says the economy's failure to go into the anticipated downspin is a direct result of people learning to stop worrying and love inflation.

Overheard at a Marketing Seminar in Charlottetown

***

GOIN' OUT RIGHT

Two brothers were born in Souris. One went away to Toronto and was doing quite well. The other stayed home and helped his dad run the family business, a corner store that barely paid its way. Eventually the day came when the father died. The brother in Souris called the one in Toronto and begged him to come home for the wake and the funeral.

"Can't do it," said Toronto, "but I want you to send him out right and then send me the bill."

After a time a bill arrived for $5,075.00 so he paid it. The next month a bill for $75.00 arrived and he also paid that, thinking it was something that had been

missed the month before. When a bill for $75.00 arrived the next month, he thought he should check it out and called his brother in Souris and asked about the funeral.

"Yup," he said, "we sent him out right nice."

"But what about these bills for $75," inquired Toronto.

"Oh that, well we buried him in a rented tuxedo."

45

Why did they bury the Islander on the hill?
Because he was dead.
Why did the Islander bury his mother under a step?
Because he wanted a stepmother.

***

What happened to the old Indian who drank too much tea.She died in her tea-pee.

***

Who were the five most constipated men in the Bible?
1. Cane - he wasn't able
2. David - heaven and earth couldn't move him
3. Moses - he had to go up to the mountain and take tablets
4. Solomon - sat on the throne for 40 days
5. Noah - only passed water for 40 days.

Sandi Gamble

***

The railway was an integral part of Island history, and was in fact a plum used to finally lure the province to join confederation. With the same unique perversity of nature that often surfaces with Islanders, the province had hosted the original meeting which led to the formation of Canada as a nation, then sat back with a wait and see attitude, refusing to go along with the consensus. P.E.I. did not in fact actually sign on the dotted line until tempted in with the promise of a ferry service and a railroad. Ironic that as I write this book both seemed to be doomed. Rail lines are being torn up and shipped to far off nations. The ferries, it is threatened, will be replaced by a bridge. Can't you imagine driving along, four and half miles from land on a cold winter day with winds blowing snow and ice making traction impossible!

The following look at the first two years of the P.E.I.R. was written by a good friend Allan Graham who lives "up west" and, along with his wife Mary, deserves much credit for his contribution to the arts, particularly the writing, publishing community.

THE FIRST TWO YEARS OF THE P.E.I.R.

Islanders traditionally take politics and religion very seriously. However, some of the political off-shoots have always been, and continue to be, fair target practice for newspaper editors and others. This article attempts to give brief coverage to some of the more humorous comments on the P.E.I.R. as found in the newspapers of 1871 and 1872.

In April 1871 the Railway Bill was passed by the Legislature. In the April l7th, 1871 issue of the Examiner, a letter appeared from a farmer living near East Point who suggested one possible benefit from the railway:

"Every old woman who lives near the depot would keep a thousand hens and would have a fortune made for herself and grandchildren while you would say Jack Robinson."

Celebrations erupted in many parts of the Island in honor of the passage of the Railway Bill. The Examiner correspondent in Georgetown described some of the celebration in that town:

"Georgetown people...last evening manifested the wildest excitement around a huge bon-fire of tar barrels and other combustibles, in full blast, on the public square, all in honor of the Railroad... all the windows in town were beautifully illuminated with candles, and as Georgetown possesses a Distillery, many a spirit was as radiant as the surrounding buildings."

The correspondent describes Georgetown on the day after the bash:

"The little town has again quietly sobered down to its usual gravity, and it is only reasonable that it should, after exploding a ten pound note in gunpowder, and a few hornpipes to ram home the charge."

Those communities not originally destined to have a railway felt quite differently about the Railway Bill. As the Examiner reports, Montague was full of malcontents, one of whom, was described as follows:

"...one Samson and a Justice of the Peace at that I hear, threatens to muster a force and tear up the track as fast as it is laid..."

In Summerside a banquet was held at Clifton House in which "the popping of the sparkling champagne during parts of the evening sounded like a feu de joie..."

The letters to the editor continued to debate the Railway. On May 8, 1871 the Examiner published a letter from a "Cousin Katie" of Charlottetown in which she attempted to give the feminine perspective on the passage of the Railway Bill. She gives the following comments on why the women of P.E.I. wanted the railway:

"...Suppose they (the gentlemen in the opposition) have a Lady Love, which I trust each one has or will have, residing about thirty or forty miles from themselves, would it not be much more pleasant for them to step on the Cars and arrive at her home, clean and neat, without one speck of this red mud being on their clothes..."

The same issue of the examiner contains a letter from a resident of Rollo Bay with a novel suggestion for financing the railway:

"Sir: I am happy to inform you that a move is being made here in the right direction, it is to agitate for a tax to be levied on all old bachelors for Railroad purposes. From here to East Point I can count about fifty of them all in a row, who are no good to themselves or anyone else...We propose to tax them IOs per year, till they get married..."

On May 15, 1871 a Charlottetown resident responded to the Rollo Bay letter writer as follows: "The Railroad man from Rollo Bay is most unreasonable in giving countenance to any scheme for imposing a Special Tax on Bachelors. The pockets of this worthy class of citizens are already drained sufficiently. The Railroad man's letter abounds with clap-trap about Bachelors that he should be ashamed of. This self-denying branch of the population should rather be paid a bounty..."

The P.E.I. Government played footsie with the tender calls for the Railway. The firm Walker & Co. of London was squeezed out of the race and Mr. W.D. O'Brien of Halifax seemed to have a strong possibility of receiving the contract to build the Railway. The P.E.I. Government managed to frustrate O'Brien's efforts. The Halifax Citizen of Sept. 9, 1871 expressed the problem as follows:

"The Government objects to Mr. W.D. O'Brien on the ground that he does not offer sufficient security. We in Halifax are included to believe that the names of Sir Edward Kenny and Charles Murdock, Esq. are sufficient security for the purchase of the whole Island, far less for the construction of a paltry railway through its interior."

By far the most humorous editorial on the early days of the P.E.I. Railway concerned the poorly-planned and executed turning of the first sod. The Patriot of October 7, 1871 contains an extensive editorial describing this "sad and sorry affair." It goes on to call the event the greatest "fizzle in the history of the colony." For most of the day the sod-turning was to take place, no one knew where and exactly when the sod would be turned. In the afternoon word was spread that it would occur at 5 o'clock that evening. This time was not suitable for farmers who had to travel home long distances — as the editor commented, "though most of our sturdy plowmen...may have seen sods turned prettily before, (they) never saw a railway sod in their lives." This editorial describes in graphic detail what transpired that afternoon on Kensington Road:

"No doubt they (the farmers) expected to behold some fair lady, with a silver spade, raise a neat little bit of turf into a mahogany wheelbarrow, and see it trundle off and deposited as the first of a mighty embankment over which the iron horse would speed at an early day. The Railway Commissioners and their masters, however, had no such sight for the gaping multitude. An old dilapidated wheelbarrow, in which an ordinary man with a common spade deposited a lump of earth, was what men and horses had seen before and only asses need care to see again...Scarcely anybody saw the sod, unless it were the youngsters who tore it to pieces, and pelted the crowd with the fragments. Nobody raised a cheer except two or three half-wits..."

After the surveyor's maps become public knowledge the public began complaining about the circuitous route. Since the contractors were paid by the mile, hills and gullies were avoided. Two quotes from the Patriot describe this problem with clarity, the first from Dec. 30, 1871, the second from Feb. 21, 1872:

"Near Hunter River, we have been credibly informed that one mile of country gives two miles and 110 yards of narrow gauge! At North River it requires three miles of railway to get one and a half miles nearer Summerside!! We believe it is somewhere in the same vicinity that the line crosses a widow's five chain farm three times!!!"

"The railway crosses roads at 11 places between Traveller's Rest and Kensington, a distance of five miles, and a very level county. It crosses the main post road four times in three miles in the same locality."

All over the neighbouring areas of Nova Scotia and New Brunswick and even further, the P.E.I. Railway was being freely debated and laughed at. The Halifax Church Chronicle did a great job of summarizing the feelings of off-Islanders re the Railway when it commented:

"It seems that some interested individuals have been applying the law of circular sailing to railroads, and have been studying how to avoid every knoll, and every slope, and thus have given the proposed line some of the most graceful curves, and in the most masterly way put an iron girdle around every hill in order to avoid tunnelling, and cutting through, we were going to the rock, but there are no rocks."

Reprinted from Canadian
Railway #372
with permission of Allan Graham

***

OVER ON THE ISLAND

Back in 1939 one Helen Jean Champion came to Prince Edward Island for the summer and proceeded to walk and/or bicycle around the province, recording her thoughts, conversations and knowledge gleaned of the history of the areas she visited in a wonderful book called "Over On The Island". Its a wonderful book, even if a hoggle poddle of rambling thoughts and experiences. The following excerpt was written when Helen and a companion, Jean, were in what they termed The Belle River Community."

"I was discussing the train service with Jean in town just before we started on our trip. Jean marvelled at the politeness of the Island trains.

"Why, do you know," she exclaimed, "the trains actually back out of Charlottetown. They back out of Montague.. ."

"And by golly," broke in a dejected-looking man sitting near us, "they back out of Elmira."

"They back out of Alberton," went on Jean, "and out of Souris.. ."

I was astounded. Such politeness with regard to trains is not experienced in every province. I called up the train dispatcher.

"Back out of Elmira?" He was genuinely shocked, "Why, miss, they couldn't."

"Well, what do they do?"

"They back in to Elmira...and in to Montague...and in to Charlottetown."

Politeness! Pouff!

There are some really classic jokes about the Island. They have descended from father to son, have been told, retold, and still are being told. Somehow, they never seem to lose their flavour, or grow old. The favourite is hoary with age. Naturally, it concerns the freight train.

Tignish is the western terminus of the railway. Shortly after the regular freight train left Charlottetown, the conductor went around the train taking up the tickets. There was only one small boy, bound for Tignish. The conductor took

his ticket, chatted with him for a while, then returned to the freight car. Hour after hour passed. Finally, after the stops at everyone's back door had been concluded, the train neared Tignish. The conductor came around again to take the tickets. Still, there was only one passenger, but this time it was an old, old man with long, silver hair and trembling hands.

"Ticket, sir," said the conductor.

"But I gave you my ticket just after we left Charlottetown."

"I beg your pardon, sir, but you weren't here then. There was only a little boy.. ."

"Aye!" said the old man sadly, "I was that little boy."

There is still another concerning the freight trains. The traveller asked the time the train was due at the terminus. The conductor handed him a calendar.

And the trains don't even run on Sundays!

Religious! Perhaps!

Over on the Island
Helen Jean Champion

***

An out-of-province visitor was pulled over by a Mountie who started to write him a speeding ticket.

"Wait officer, you can't give me a ticket I never speed," cried the visitor.

"Oh yeah," replied the Mountie, "so how come you have a fuzz buster on the dash of your car?"

"Well officer," explained the visitor, "when I come into a new town I like to be able to find out where the donut shops are."

***

A Texan visiting P.E.I. stopped to chat with a farmer mending fences. The Texan asked how big the farm was, but when told it went up the following fence line was not impressed.

"At home I can get in my car and sit there all day without getting to the other side of my property," he bragged.

"Gee, too bad. I used to have car like that too," sympathized the farmer.

53

A huge motor home pulled into the campground, impressing everyone with its luxurious attachments. On the front was a licence plate reading,
Lee Pong
Retirement
Home
On the back with a license plate that read,
Keep
Off

***

A tourist was getting really tired of his kids who seemed to be constantly complaining and asking to buy things, but would never pay attention when their parents spoke or even enjoy the things the family was doing. Finally he told them both off.

"You have to remember, God gave you two ears and one mouth," he stormed. "Maybe there is a reason for that."

***

JOB DESCRIPTION

How many sportscasters does it take to screw in a light bulb?

Three - One to screw it in, one to do a play-by-play description, and one to do analysis.

Frank Cameron CBC News

U.F.O. SIGHTING

Early risers in Riverdale thought for a few minutes they had seen a U.F.O. (unidentified flying object) early this morning.

"I was coming back from the bathroom about 5 a.m., looked out the bedroom window and there was suddenly a bright yellow/gold light hovering over just above the horizon.

It was weird, looking through the screen turned it into a four point star, quite lovely, but strange how it hovered like it did," said Julie Watson.

Then suddenly it was joined by another. Minutes later the first disappeared, then a third appeared slightly above and to the north of the other two. At least north from where we were observing them, looking over the Bonshaw Hills."

Mrs. Watson and her husband Jack finally decided it could only be flares, dropped from a plane and a quick call to the RCMP confirmed that it was indeed flares being used in the search for a lost boat off Victoria shore.

Going back to bed Mrs. Watson informed her husband, Jack, that it was indeed falres, "Darn, I was hoping it was U.F.O.'s," said Mrs. Watson, plunking

the camera, and its roll of film shot off as 'evidence', down on the dresser, I could have written the book and got rich."

"Well dear, it was a U.F.O. till you called the Mounties and found out what they were," yawned her husband. "Now be quiet so I can get another half hours sleep."

***

OVERHEARD

The C.O.T.C. instructor was leading his class through the maze of military science and an officer cadet was becoming, to say the very least, extremely bored. As he gazed out the open door the figure of a Lieutenant caught his eye. As he hurried by he yawned mightily.

Suddenly the cadet raised his hand and spoke: "Sir, I think you're being overheard in the corridor."

Red & White, Winter '5l

***

MIND GAMES

Two contingents of the Militia, one from Charlottetown and the other from Summerside, were involved in manoeuvres in the Bonshaw Hills. The Summerside group went to their commander and said they didn't have enough guns to go around. In his most smarting military voice the commander told them to pretend they had guns.

"Yell bang when you sight the Townies and tell them they're out of the action," he commanded.

Confident that his troops would make him proud the Commander took up a position to survey the games but was horrified at what he saw.

"I told you to go and take that hill," he screeched at his second in command.

"We can't sire," cried the young fellow, who was still wet behind the ears, "Look!"

The leader looked up to see the Charlottetown boys break over the hill, chanting, "Tank! Tank! Tank!"

***

BANG, BANG

That one reminded me of the time we held a competitive trail ride in the Bonshaw Hills. The military were playing war the same weekend and unfortunately used the same colour markers as we had.

Our riders were continually surprised by young soldiers popping up and "shooting" them.

I'm sure the Militia troops thought they had stepped back in time to the days of horse mounted infantry.

***

During a bi-service parade in which members of the COTC and the UNTD participated, the army officer in charge shouted to the UNTD boys: "Stand at attention!"

"We are at attention, Sir," was the murmur, "it's our uniforms that are at ease."

Red & White, Winter '53

***

OOPS!

An enlisted man up in Summerside had a bad habit of going to the mess when he got off duty and drinking until he was "hammered". His wife had had enough of this behavior and went to the base chaplain to tell him she had decided to leave her husband. He convinced her that her husband was not an evil man, but needed help to straighten his life out. She, said the chaplain, must give him reason to improve his life, and tender loving care to ensure that she would stick with him through the difficult times that lay ahead if he were to stop drinking.

The talk had reminded the wife of the early days of their marriage and she decided that she too had been negligent. Determined that they should work together to solve their problems she shopped for a new negligee, brought new perfume and even got her hair done in a fancy new style. When he came home, worse for the wear as usual, she ignored his inebriated state and welcomed him with a big kiss. Then she led him to the living room where she helped him out of his jacket, loosened his tie and brought him his favourite meal. While he ate she nibbled his ear and whispered sweet nothings in his ear. When he finished his meal, she folded his napkin and in her most seductive voice urged him to go upstairs, to bed.

"We may as well," he sighed, "I'm gonna be killed when I get home anyway!"

***

KEEPING HIS STRENGTH UP

The newly married young sailor came in for some ribbing when he returned to his ship after his honeymoon, particularly from one macho lieutenant who thought himself exceptional in the romance department and bragged about his conquests frequently. The newlywed took all the jokes in good humour but one day turned the scales.

At breakfast he nonchalantly asked the lieutenant, and everyone else at the table, "Do you know what the world's greatest lover has for breakfast?"

None of his listeners could hazard a guess. "Well let's see," pondered the young man. "On Sunday I had bacon and eggs, on Monday I had bacon, eggs and homefries, on Tuesday, I had.............."

***

COLD WEATHER GEAR

One cold winter morning I was running late and had to speed up my usual routine so that I wouldn't be late for a meeting. I washed my hair, ran a comb through, threw on my coat and gloves and dashed for the car. By the time I reached the car, parked down at the road because of drifting snow, my hair had frozen solid - and I had my very own "hard hat".

***

And then there is Stanley who defies the dictates of fashion and always switches to light greys and winter whites with the first snow fall.

"Beegeezers if I's gonna ruin me good navies boy-oh with Ghiz's highway-men doozing tha roads wi salt," he explained.

***

FACTS RIGHT

A country dweller, listening to the weather forecast on CBC Radio heard the announcer say the weather was still and clear. Looking out the window he turned to his wife and growled, "Aye, they've got that right the snows still falling and its clear up to your ass."

***

OVERHEARD AT THE
WOMEN IN BUSINESS CONFERENCE

Definition of a man's bald head: Solar panel for a sex machine.

A newly-married career woman was discussing the ramifications of having children with a working mom of three. The obvious question came up and the mother of three was asked if she would have children again if she could do it all over again.

"Oh sure," she said, "Just not the same ones."

***

Of a local know-it-all who always seemed to start her friendly, but very unwelcome offerings of advice with, "I hope you don't mind my telling you this,"......it's a darn sure thing you will.

***

Of the move to input all data in an office to computers and eliminate the old filing cabinets: "I don't know about this, I really liked shuffling papers."

***

If a mother wants some time alone all she has to do is the dishes.

***

I have good manners. Thats all that keeps me from telling her what bad manners she has!

***

LIFE'S LITTLE PLEASURES

Coming out of a long running meeting at the Chamber of Commerce and find no parking ticket on the car.

***

SAID IN CONFERENCE

"I've always wanted those fancy initials behind my name," I complained to a friend when attending a conference that seemed too prolific in academic types for my peace of mind.

"Well, now its official, you've finally got some," said my friend, "Julie V. Watson, CFA."

"CFA," I questioned, "What's that?"

"Came from away," was the reply.

***

The owner of a ladies wear store in Summerside was relating how she developed her career to women attending a conference in that town. "I only wish I had known what I know now, 10 years ago; would have had more energy and fewer hot flashes."

***

ON SUCCESS

To sell it you usually have to go that extra smile.

***

SIGNS IN MY OFFICE....

We Are Always PROMPT........No Matter How Long It Takes

CHAOS is our business

I'm PERFECTLY ADJUSTED so don't fool around with the knobs...

You think you've got problems?
I'm so far behind....Tomorrow is gone before I even get there!

***

THE WOMAN'S VIEW

Two women were talking during a coffee break were feeling disgruntled about their spouses. One the oldest said, "Mine's retired, now I have twice the husband and half the money."

The other, younger and a mother of small children, said "that's bad, but not as bad as mine. He told the children that Santa comes from Tignish because only someone from Tignish would be dumb enough to squeeze down a chimney when the house is full of doors and windows."

Another woman, seeking to lighten the conversation asked the two if the knew what was long and hard on an Island man. When they both replied "no," she smiled and said, "Grade 3."

WHOSE POCKET?

An aftermath of horse races on Summerside harbour ice one Saturday in late February, was the great number of intoxicated men to be seen around the streets. During the late afternoon a series of scuffles attracted large crowds. A few blows were struck but nothing very serious developed. One of those involved who had been displaying a large roll of bills complained that it had in some mysterious way disappeared.

Journal Pioneer Flashback to February 28, 1927

***

An English Professor, an apostle of the "Return to the land Movement", was lecturing to his class.

"A lot of people," he said, "talk about returning to the land, but not many of them ever do. NOW, I not only advocate it but I intend to do just that. Why, even now I know what the farmers do. The other day I saw a man building a horse. He had the horse almost finished; he was just nailing on the back feet as I came in."

Red & White, Winter '53

***

A SHRINKING AFFAIR

A few years ago I read of a man who, for some reason, made traces, to be used when hitching up his horses for work, out of eelskin. The tale went that eelskin was more readily available than leather and plentiful.

Well the man in question was out hauling wood home for the winter when the traces - or the eelskins began to stretch, presumably because they got wet - or something. Now I'm told the sleigh bogged down, but the horse kept going till eventually the sleigh was out of sight. The driver and horse arrived home, plum tuckered from slogging through the bush and he decided to rest awhile before going back for the sleigh. While they were inside the house, the weather turned dry, a breeze came up and the eelskin shrunk back to its original size. The horse being tied, stayed where it was and the shrinking traces delivered the load of wood right to the door.

***

SCHOOL HUMOUR

In 1904 The Prince Edward Island Magazine ran a series of articles entitled, An Educational Outlook. Most of the material was serious stuff. A look at the education system and the people involved with it, both at home and away. But each issue also had an offering of School Humour, some of which we repeat here:

The Reason Why:

Father - "Why don't you sit down?"
Son - "This morning I asked you "how many made a million, and you said: 'Damn few.' I told the teacher that in arithmetic class to-day, an that's why I can't sit down."

In A Twentieth Century School:

Q" - If a father gave nineteen cents to one of his sons, and six cent to the other, what time would it be?
A. - Why, a quarter to two, of course.

Q - If a post master went to a menagerie and was eaten up by one of the wild beasts, what would be the hour?
A. - Nothing could be easier. Eight P.M.

Q - If a guest at a restaurant ordered a lobster and ate it and another guest did the same, what would be the second guests telephone number?
A. - Absurdly simple, 8-1-2.

A Tired Voice:

The children had written a composition on the giraffe. They were reading them aloud to the class. At length the time came for little Willie to read his. It was as follows:

"The giraffe is a dumb animal and cannot express itself by any sound, because its neck is so long that its voice gets tired on its way to its mouth."

Sir Walter's Successor:

This story is told of Sir Walter Scott who was far from being a brilliant pupil at school. After he became famous he one day dropped into the old school to pay a visit to the scene of his former woes. The teacher was anxious to make a good impression on the visitor, and put the pupils through their lesson so as to show them to the best advantage. After a while Scott said: "But which is the dunce? You have one surely? Show him to me." The teacher called up a poor fellow who looked the picture of woe, as he bashfully came toward the distinguished visitor. "Are you the dunce?" asked Scott. "Yes, sir," said the boy. "Well my good fellow," said Scott, "Here is a crown for you for keeping my place warm."

A New Definition:

"How is the earth divided?" asked a Summerside teacher a few weeks ago.
"By earthquakes, sir" was the prompt answer from one of the most eager of the pupils.

In The Style:

A school boy upon being asked by his teacher how he should flog him, replied, "If you please, sir, I should like to have it on the style of penmanship, the heavy strokes upward and the downward ones light."

A Fish Story:

Mother - Johnny, you said you'd been to a Sunday School?
Johnny - (with a far away look) - Yes im.
Mother - How does it happen that your hands smell fishy?
Johnny - I carried home the Sunday School paper, an the outside page is all about Jonah and the whale.

A Genus Homo, Species Man:

Here is a bright little school girl's composition on men: "Men are what women marry: They drink and smoke and swear and have ever so many pockets, but they won't go to church. Perhaps if they wore bonnets they would. They are more logical than women and always were zoological. Both men and women have sprung from monkeys, but the women certainly sprung further than the men."

Essay on Man:

The following is an extract from a real composition written by a small schoolboy in New Jersey. The subject given by the teacher was the extensive one of "Man."

Here's what the small boy wrote: "Man is a wonderful animal. He has eyes, ears, mouth. His ears are mostly for catching cold and having the earache. The nose is to get snuffles with. A man's body is split halfway up and he walks on the split ends."

An Easy plan

A young man once wrote to Beecher saying "I am an honest young man and I would like an easy place. "Beecher replied, "Don't be an editor, don't be a minister, don't be a lawyer, a mechanic or a civil engineer, don't be a teacher, in fact don't be anything, for the only easy place is in Greenwood Cemetery."

In Full Dress:

Little Alice, three years old, was dressed by her Auntie, in low neck and short sleeves. She stood for a moment looking at her bars, then she exclaimed, "Auntie, my mamma don't love my arms to go barefooted."

The Reason Why:

Mrs. Wackum. - "How did that naught boy of yours hurt himself?"
Mrs. Snapper. - "That good little boy of yours hit him on the head with a brick.

Tommy's worry:

Four year-old Tommy had listened with great attention to his mother's story of how Eve had been created from one of Adam's ribs. "And didn't it hurt, mamma," asked Tommy, with a grave far-away look.

"Well, it may have hurt, some" was mamma's answer, "but Adam never murmured."

The next day Tommy complained of a pain. "Where is the pain dear," asked his mother.

It's in my side, mamma," said Tommy, tearfully, "and I jest spects I'm going to have a wife."

THE SUFFRAGETTE

Be to her virtues very kind
Be to her faults a little blind
Let all her ways be unconfined
And clap your padlock on her mind.

The Charlottetown Examiner January 2nd, 1914

***

"Before we were married, Henry," said the young wife reproachfully, "you always gave me the most beautiful Christmas presents. Do you remember?"
"Sure," said Henry cheerfully, "but my dear, did you ever hear of a fisherman giving bait to a fish after he caught it."

The Charlottetown Examiner February l9th, 1914

***

THE BACKBONE

Though beauty and youth may have flown
Rare is the woman who can't hold her own,
If it comes to a show-down
She'll stick on a low-gown
Just to show she still has some backbone.

The Charlottetown Examiner February l8th, 1914

***

FIXED LINK

One enterprising Island old timer was shocked when he heard about the proposed millions of dollars going to be spent to provide the Island with a fixed link to the mainland.

He went down to see the premier and suggested that a contract be given to he and his son, who would each start digging a tunnel from opposite sides of the Northumberland Strait for a fraction of the cost being proposed by huge contracting firms.

"And what happens if your calculations are out and you don't meet in the middle," asked the skeptical Premier.

"Well then lad, you gets two tunnels," was the reply.

***

Another old timer is skeptical about the idea of being out so far from shore, especially during stormy weather and wants to know if life jackets will be issued to those driving over the link.

***

TOUGH LUCK

Our idea of tough luck is that of the chap who wore a pair of old, tattered gloves for two months before Christmas and then had to go out and buy himself a new pair.

***

NEW NEWS

"That's a fine, imposing building over there on the corner of Kent and Queen Streets."

"Right you are! And it contains a fine-imposing magistrate. Its the police court.

The local householder can now get a chance to try his hand at snow-shovelling no matter how much he doesn't want to.

The Charlottetown Examiner January 10th, 1914

The recent snow storm showed that those people who neglected to shovel their sidewalks all winter have not been smitten with any noticeable degree of remorse at the last.

The Charlottetown Examiner April 4th, 1914

THE DIFFERENCE BETWEEN........

Dogs and cats is......dogs come when called; cats take a message and get back to you

Genius and Stupidity is.......that genius has its limits

Antiques and Junk is........who's running the flea market

Fast and Gourmet Burgers is.......about ten bucks

Past and Future is........the past gives us experiences and memories; the present gives us challenges and opportunities; and the future gives us hope.

***

CAUTION

"Ain't you rather young to be left in charge of a drugstore?"

"Perhaps; what can I do for you?"

"Do your employers know it's dangerous to leave a mere boy like you in charge of such a place?"

"I am competent to serve you madam, if you will state your wants."

"Don't they know you might poison someone?"

"There is no danger of that, madam; what can I do for you?" "Think I better go to the store down the street."

"I can serve you just as well as they can, and as cheaply." "Well, you may give me a two cent stamp, but it don't look right."

The Charlottetown Examiner January 7th, 1914

***

A tree never hits a car, except in self-defense.

Sign of the Times at Movie World.

A pro-lifer asked the priest when life began. The priest said at conception.

The pro-lifer asked a rabbi and he said, "when the kids are gone and the dog is dead."

Michael

***

REEKING DELIVERY

Rural mail delivery is an integral part of Island life, and often generates rib tickling incidents.

Ernie and Margaret Affleck held the Savage Harbour route for 53 years and retired with many fond memories which the related to Guardian reporter Kent Walker. One particular incident resulted from the habit residents had years ago of shipping liquor to each other as gifts through the mail. One time some of the liquor spilled over some newspapers. Mr. Affleck asked the postmaster what was to be done with the papers and she said to deliver them, so deliver them he did. Needless-to-say the recipient was not impressed to receive his papers reeking of liquor!

***

LOGIC

"The train struck the man, did it not?" asked the lawyer of the engineer at the trial.
"It did, sir," said the engineer.
"Was the man on the track, sir?" thundered the lawyer.
"On the track?" asked the engineer. "Of course he was. No engineer would run his train into the woods after a man - sir."

The Charlottetown Examiner February l9th, 1914

CURE FOR EXHAUSTION

Sometimes, exhausted
with toil and endeavor,
I wish I could sleep
for ever and ever;

but then this reflection
my longing allays!
I shall be doing it
one of these days.

***

T.T.T.

Put up in a place where it's easy to see the cryptic admonishment T.T.T.
When you feel how depressingly slowly you climb,its well to remember,
Things Take Time!

Among treasured pieces
I've had for years....and years.

***

Marriage, like life, is hard by the yard
By the inch, its a cinch.

***

Two ants were running along at a great rate across a cracker box.
"Why are you going so fast," asked one."Don't you see?" said the other. "It
says, 'tear along dotted line'."

Red & White, Winter '49

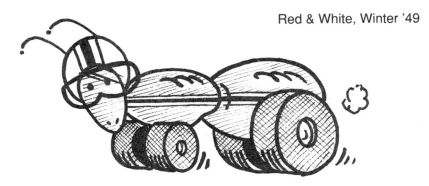

ALL IN ONE

While shopping for vacation clothes the husband and wife passed a display of bathing suits. It had been years - and 20 pounds - since the wife had even considered buying a bathing suit but since her husband had pressured her to join the fitness club with him, she sought his advice on the purchase.

"What do you think," she asked, "Should I get a bikini or an all-in-one?"
"Better get the bikini," he replied, "You'd never get it all in one."

***

After 25 years of happy marriage the couple had rented a cottage up near Stanhope. The wife was feeling right passionate when they finished watching an romantic old movie on the late show.

With her most provocative smile she looked up at her hubby and whispered, "Honey. How about carrying me off to bed?" "Only if I can make two trips," he replied.

***

SIGNS OF THE TIMES

A group of dentists is known as - a drill team.
Life is like a dog sled team - Unless you're the lead dog the view never changes.
If life gives you lemons - Make lemonade.

Kevin's Car Wash.

***

Did you hear about the Island gal who won a gold medal at the Olympics? Her parents were so proud they rushed right out and had it bronzed!

Charlottetown Chamber of Commerce

***

You gotta match?
Not since Superman died.

***

What has twelve paws and two wheels?
Three bears on a bicycle.

Leah Fraser, New Glasgow

77

After a pre-election rally two farmers were discussing the merits of a candidates speech: "How long did he speak?"
"About an hour and a half."
"And what was it all about?"
"He didn't say."

***

A civil servant is described as a caboose with delusions of being a locomotive.

***

The road to hell is paved with good intentions. In Prince Edward Island, so are the potholes.

***

Bumper sticker seen in Ottawa: "Love is Where you Fund it."

***

You can declare yourself an adult Canadian when you no longer believe in Santa Claus, the Easter Bunny, and deficit reduction.

A Summerside girl was trying to swim the 11 km across the Strait. She got out 6 km and realized she couldn't make it so turned around and swam home.

***

THOSE BOYS IN BLUE

Back in the days when I was editing Charlottetown Monthly Magazine we ran an article on activities of the members of Britain's Royal Air Force who came to Prince Edward Island to train during World War II. The airmen and trainers, the local volunteers and citizens who played host to them were all influenced by that indomitable British spirit which found humour where many others would not.

Now to appreciate the Islander's involvement in the war effort you must be aware that they have always enthusiastically offered a high quota of men and women to the fighting services in times of war. A large contingent of volunteers went overseas in the South African War, and in World War I some 18% of the male population joined the march to victory. As early as 1942 over 12% of the Island population, almost 25% of the males, had already enlisted, with women also falling into line to lead the Dominion in enlistment on the basis of per capita population. Indeed, in all aspects of the major effort, P.E.I. was acknowledged as playing a foremost part.

Understanding that commitment to the military effort, it becomes easy to understand the close relationship that developed between Islanders and The Boys In Blue.

These humorous bits and pieces taken from GRAF, the base magazine put out by the RAF during their time on the Island, will hopefully bring back a memory, and perhaps a good giggle.

HEARTS AGLOW

Last night I held a little hand,
So dainty and so neat,
I thought my heart would surely burst,
So wildly did it beat.

No other hands ever held so tight,
Could greater gladness bring.
It was (the hand I held last night)
Four aces and a king.

79

GORTY
(TWO FOR THE SCOTS)

The height of meanness — Sandy going alone on his honeymoon.

If you give a Scotsman enough rope, he'll smoke it.

***

The Y.M.C.A. was an integral part of life for servicemen. As just one of the many volunteer services it served to bring locals and enlisted man together. They had their own column in GRAF.

"Perhaps the brightest note to be sounded in the 'Y' during the month came from an arm-chair generalissimo (A.C.I somebody or another) who on listening to a broadcast by a so-called war expert chirped his opinion of that person with the following brainstorm:
"That fellow's no expert." "He's the kind of bloke who looks into the gun before or after it's fired and calls himself and expert." He went on: "A true expert is the chap who looks into the gun when it is actually being fired, but unfortunately his findings and impressions are lost in the noise of the firing."

***

PADRE'S PAGES

The Chaplain's office reminds one of an elevator with its up and downs of life, its flow of humanity, with its joys an sorrows. The nature of the work is akin to parish work in many ways, and looked upon by the Church as an extension of the Church in another field. As well as tending the soul they injected a little humour reminding soldiers of the funny side of life.

"PRAISE THE LORD AND PASS UP THE BLANKETS - A fine Christian woman had the habit of saying out aloud when something in the sermon helped her, "Praise the Lord."
The Minister was irritated and so he decided on a plan of action, he kindly explained to the good woman how it disturbed him while he was preaching and promised to give her a pair of fine blankets which she needed for her family.
She did her best to refrain for a long time until a visiting preacher was holding forth with great zeal that stirred her soul so much that she at last shouted out with great joy, "Blankets or no Blankets. Praise the Lord."

J.M. Cameron, S/Ldr. C. of E. Padre

***

Flight Mechanic Chippingstead
Worked always standing on his head.
His aeroplane made pilots frown
By flying only upside down.

"Intelligent fellers
Don't walk into propellers." VEEBLOCK

***

HOW TO FLY A BOMBER

In Two Easy Lessons

LESSON NO. 1

(I) Find the most comfortable seat in the bomber, that's the pilot's

(II) Sit down, turn on all knobs and switches you can see, shouting out to whoever may be listening, "Contact", "Switches off", "Tea up" and "All together, Boys". If nothing happens ask the fitter where the petrol-cocks are kept, his answer will probably be "I don't know, possibly with hens in the Hen-coop."

(III) In this case find another bomber and repeat operations (I and II).

(IV) As soon as the engine starts seize the control-column and sink into a trance.

(V) While in the trance you may hear a certain noise, if it is a loud report preceded by a sinking feeling you will know that you have turned one of the taps, switches or knobs the wrong way, and consequently retracted the undercarriage. The particular tap, switch or knob can be determined by the 'Trial and Error Method' using other bombers in the vicinity for Mastery of the said subject.

LESSON NO. 2

You are now in the air — do not be alarmed — whatever else happens you are bound to return, sooner or later, to the ground.

There are two ways of flying a bomber,

(I) The right way up.

(II) The wrong way up.

The latter is more novel, but not so pleasant. It can be ascertained which of the two you have adopted by a simple experiment of the watch and chain method, if the watch hangs from the ceiling all is well, if, on the other hand, it hangs from the floor, something must be wrong.

Assuming that you are the wrong way up and standing on the ceiling of the bomber. Return your watch and chain to your pocket and swing to and fro on the control column, if you are heavy enough something is bound to happen and you will find yourself standing in the bomb-bay.

Return to the pilot's seat and once more turn on all taps, switches and knobs you can see. You are now ready to land, which is very simple and requires no instruction.

D.H.M. April, 1943

CORN OFF THE COB

(a titillation from the final issue of GRAF-Charlottetown)

An airman's wife in London received a cable from her husband in Canada: "Darling please divorce me. I am in love with a girl over here."

She cabled back: "What has she got that I haven't?" and received the short reply: "Nothing, but she's got it here."

***

Two young evacuees from England spent their Christmas on a farm. The older one woke up during the night and saw that Santa had left each stocking half-full of presents. Getting up quietly he emptied the younger one's stocking into his own tiptoed out to the barnyard and filled the stocking up with fertilizer. At breakfast Christmas morning the farmer asked the boys what they had received from Santa. The older boy enumerated all his presents with great gusto. The farmer, a bit astonished, asked the younger boy what he had received. The boy burst into tears and sobbed: "I got what I always wanted, sir. A real horse, but it must have escaped."

Back Pay

Prune was highly elated. From now on he would be known as Flying Officer Prune.

"Good show," booms the wingy.

"Atta boy Prune," cries the mess.

Under the circumstances there was nothing else to do but offer a Celebration to all and sundry.

At the height of the party a F/Lt. who had over indulged waved a copy of the "Gazette" in his hand.

"I shay old man," he remarked with difficulty, "why didn't you tell us ?" He pointed unsteadily to a column of type.

With an effort Prune focussed his eyes on the paper and found an announcement to the effect that he had been promoted w. e. f. December 21st, 942.

There you are," shouted the F/L, "been a flying officer all these years and told no one."

"Didn't know myself, old man," grinned Prune, "wonder how much back pay I'm due for."

"Back pay," repeated the F/L., "you know what these people are like over credit and that sort of thing. I'd write to them."

So then and there Prune penned a letter to H.M. Under Sec. of State for Air demanding back pay as from the year 942.

The following morning he awoke with a bad head and a fervent hope that he hadn't really posted that ridiculous letter.

A month passed—two months, and one day a letter arrived for 'Prune' marked: CONFIDENTIAL—OHMS.

With trembling fingers he sliced open the envelope. He read: "Your claim for back pay as from the year 942 in accordance with your promotion as promulgated in the Gazette has been investigated and it is agreed that this back pay is due to you. The exact amount cannot be computed owing to lack of knowledge of the rates of pay during these years. However, the Air Ministry have agreed to the sum of £30,000 in settlement of your claim". Signed F/L. Crayston.

"Struth !" yelled Prune, "look at this. " The mess crowded round and read the letter with awe.

"Gawd," gasped the Doc, "what a party we'll have. Hold on though, there's more on the back."

They turned over and read on.

"During the investigation it has come to light that during the period 1140 to 1206 a large quantity of material consisting of horses, chariots, bows, arrows and BSA crossbows were missing from H.M. Government's Service Stores. As you are the only living officer who held rank at that time it has been considered necessary that you be held responsible for these losses. We were fortunate to find in the account an accurate estimate which valued the missing equipment at £30,003: 16: 4 1/2d. If you will forward a cheque for the odd £3: 16:4 1/2d we shall be deeply grateful for your patriotic gesture in demanding an investigation and will be prepared to consider the matter closed."

Endeth The Humour Section.

(Spring, 1951)

GOOD THINGS A LEARN

Learn to laugh. A good laugh is better than medicine.

Learn to attend strictly to your own business. Very important point.

Learn how to tell a story. A well told story is as welcome as a sunbeam in a sickroom.

Learn to stop croaking. If you cannot see any good in the world, keep the bad to yourself.

Learn to keep your own troubles to yourself. The world is too busy to care for your ills and sorrows.

Learn to greet your friends with a smile. They carry too many frowns in their own hearts to be bothered by any of yours.

Learn to hide your aches and pains under a pleasant smile. No one cares whether you have the earache, stomach ache or a pain in your big toe.

The Prince Edward Island Magazine - 1904

- The End -